MW00619592

IN MARY'S ARMS

IN MARY'S ARMS

A Christmas Message for Mothers

MARY HOLLAND McCANN

DESERET
BOOK

SALT LAKE CITY, UTAH

Book design © Deseret Book Company.
Art direction: Richard Erickson. Book design: Sheryl Dickert Smith.

Cover painting: Madonna and Child (oil on canvas), Sassoferrato, Il (Giovanni Battista Salvi) (1609–85)/Palazzo Ducale, Urbino, Italy/Bridgeman Images.

Cover and interior decorative images: Shutterstock © Nata_Tata and Shutterstock © Kozyrina Olga

DESERET BOOK is a registered trademark of Deseret Book Company.

Visit us at DeseretBook.com

Library of Congress Cataloging-in-Publication Data

Names: McCann, Mary Holland, 1969– author.
Title: In Mary's arms : a Christmas message for mothers / Mary Holland McCann.
Description: Salt Lake City, Utah : Deseret Book, [2016] | Includes bibliographical references.
Identifiers: LCCN 2016021148 | ISBN 9781629722450 (hardbound : alk. paper)
Subjects: LCSH: Mary, Blessed Virgin, Saint. | Christmas. | Motherhood—Religious aspects—Christianity.
Classification: LCC BT603 .M43 2016 | DDC 232.91—dc23
LC record available at https://lccn.loc.gov/2016021148

Printed in the United States of America
Edwards Brothers Malloy, Ann Arbor, MI

10 9 8 7 6 5 4 3 2

CONTENTS

And he shall be called Jesus Christ, the Son of God, the Father of heaven and earth, the Creator of all things from the beginning; and his mother shall be called Mary.

—MOSIAH 3:8

A SACRED
RESPONSIBILITY

A few years ago, I read a newspaper article about a bus driver who reported that a pregnant woman probably somewhere in her mid-thirties got on his bus wearing no shoes. It was bitter cold outside, and she wore only a ragged coat and torn socks. She explained that she had boarded the bus to warm up, even though it was headed in the direction opposite of where she needed to go. Her money, she said, would stretch to cover shoes for her eight children, but she didn't have enough to buy a pair for herself.

During the course of their conversation, a teenage boy got up to exit the bus. The driver reported, "That kid walked up with his shoes in his hand and just handed them to the woman. He was barefoot. Imagine giving your shoes to someone else on a day like that. He just looked at her and said, 'Here, lady, you need these more than me.'" Overwhelmed by the boy's selfless gesture, the woman began to cry. The bus driver cried with her.

When he was asked about it later, the boy's explanation of his behavior was simple but profound: "I felt sorry for her. It was very cold out and she looked really worn. I figured we'll probably always have enough money to get shoes. She'll probably never have enough. It was nothing. After all," he said, "it's Christmas" ("Teen Bares Feet to Shoe Woman," *Deseret News*, 1984).

What is it that prompts people to act like this during Christmas? What makes a teenage boy walk up to a stranger, hand her the shoes he is wearing, and in explanation simply reply, "It's Christmas"? I believe we feel this swell of generosity because during the season in which we celebrate Christ's birth, we want to be more like Him. We feel almost compelled to try to live the way He lived—selflessly and generously and sometimes even in bare feet.

So, how did Jesus Christ come to be who He was? How did He come to embody these attributes that we try so hard at Christmastime (and should try all the time) to emulate? He is who He is because He is a God. Modern-day scripture reveals John's witness of Jesus Christ's divinity: "And he bore record, saying: I saw his glory, that he was in the beginning, before the world was; . . . The light and the Redeemer of the world; . . . who came into the world, because the world was made by him, and in him was the life of men and the light of men. The worlds were made by him; men were made by him; all things were made by him, and through him, and of him. And I, John, bear record that I beheld his glory, as the glory of the Only Begotten of the Father, full of grace and truth, even the Spirit of truth, which came and dwelt in the flesh, and dwelt among us" (D&C 93:7–11). Jesus Christ is the literal Son of God and, by divine right, a God Himself.

However, as John teaches, He is a God who chose to take on the flesh of mortality and to live among us. He intentionally chose to become mortal in order to experience what we experience, to feel how we feel, and to live and die as we do so that not only would He be able to save us when we die but He would know how to succor and sustain us while we live. He received the gift of mortality from His mother, Mary. Elder James E. Talmage taught, "In His nature would be combined the powers of Godhood with the capacity and possibilities of mortality; and this through the ordinary operation of the fundamental law of heredity. . . . The Child Jesus was to inherit the physical, mental, and spiritual traits, tendencies, and powers that characterized His parents—one immortal and glorified—God, the other human—[Mary]." (*Jesus the Christ* [1983], 77).

Given that unique combination of inherited traits, what would His mortal experience have been like? John continues to teach that in terms of growth and development, it would have been very much like ours. He states, "And I, John, saw that [Jesus Christ] received not of the fulness at the first, but received grace for grace; . . . until he received a fulness; and thus he was called the Son of God, because he received not of the fulness at the first" (D&C 93:12–14). Luke likewise teaches of Jesus' natural, mortal development by speaking of Him "increas[ing] in wisdom and stature, and in favour with God and man" (Luke 2:52).

Elder Talmage further explains Christ's mortal development: "In such simplicity is the normal, natural development of the Boy Jesus made clear. He came among men to experience all the natural conditions of mortality; He was born as truly a dependent, helpless babe as is any other child; His infancy was in all common features as the infancy of others; His boyhood was actual boyhood, His development was as necessary and as real as that of all children. Over His mind had fallen the veil of forgetfulness common to all who are born to earth, by which the remembrance of primeval existence is shut off. The Child grew, and with growth there came to Him expansion of mind, development of faculties, and progression in power and understanding" (*Jesus the Christ,* 105).

Heavenly Father knew Jesus would have to experience mortality, grow from "grace to grace," and increase in mind, body, and spirit. With that in mind, He chose Mary to be His mother. Elder Bruce R. McConkie says of Mary's foreordained call: "As there is only one Christ, so there is only one Mary. And as the Father chose the most noble and righteous of all his spirit sons to come into mortality as his Only Begotten in the flesh, so we may confidently conclude that he selected the most worthy and spiritually talented of all his spirit daughters to be the mortal mother of his Eternal Son" (*Doctrinal New Testament Commentary*, 3 vols. [1965], 1:85).

Mary would have been the one to teach Jesus to walk and talk. She would have been the one to dry His tears and to smile when He laughed. Hers would have been the face He first saw expressing the love of God. She would have been the one to teach Him the scriptures and how to pray. She, directed by Elohim, was called upon to nurture the Savior of the world.

Robert J. Matthews wrote: "When we consider the strong influence that a mother has on the personality and attitude of a young child in the home, we sense the responsibility that our Heavenly Father gave Mary by entrusting her with the rearing of his chosen and Beloved Son" ("Mary and Joseph," *Ensign*, December 1974). What mortal woman is capable of such responsibility? I am a mother of five earthly children, and I feel that my responsibility to raise them in righteousness is nearly overwhelming. Too many nights I go to bed in tears wondering how I can possibly measure up. I cannot imagine Mary's mission. What was it about her that made her capable of such responsibility? Why did He choose Mary?

We don't have a great deal of information about

Mary. We have a few verses from the Nativity story, the marriage at Cana, and a scene at the Savior's Crucifixion. Each of these encounters deserves its own study. However, as we celebrate Christmas, it is fitting to study what we can about Mary in the Nativity story and determine what characteristics qualified her for her tremendous calling.

And the angel came
in unto her, and said,
Hail, thou that art
highly favoured,
the Lord is with thee:
blessed art thou
among women.

—LUKE 1:28

REPLACING FEAR WITH FAITH

The Gospel of Luke gives us the only account we have of Gabriel's visit to Mary. It reads, "And the angel came in unto her, and said, Hail, thou that art highly favoured, the Lord is with thee: blessed art thou among women. And when she saw him, she was troubled at his saying, and cast in her mind what manner of salutation this should be. And the angel said unto her, Fear not, Mary: for thou hast found favour with God" (Luke 1:28–30). It is not insignificant that the first thing we learn about Mary is that she was afraid. Probably somewhere in her early teens, she would surely have been no less "troubled" to be visited by an angel than you or I would be. Undoubtedly, that was why after Gabriel greeted her, one of the first things he told her was to "fear not." She was afraid, and he knew it. Mary, foreordained before the world was formed, chosen by God, and destined for greatness, was afraid. What distinguishes her is that she went headlong into her fear and found her faith. She asked only one question of the angel, which was to wonder how this could be possible inasmuch as she was still a virgin. This innocent, sweet question only illustrated what little she knew of her mission, the power of God, and what lay ahead. But, with her question answered, she squared her chin and followed her faith.

I love the faith Mary showed here, but I love even more that she found it in the midst of her fear.

The story wouldn't be the same for me if she were more confident—because it simply wouldn't seem real. To be the mortal mother of the Son of God, Mary would have been full of human emotions, including fear. However, she would also have to be one who would never allow that, or any other emotion, to deter her faith. She would have to be a mother who could teach her son that nothing (including fear) can keep you from honoring God's will.

Like Mary, every mother feels some fear as we are called upon to bear and raise children. We might be afraid we aren't smart enough, good enough, or talented enough. We might be afraid that we are too strict when we should be merciful, and then on another day that we are too merciful when we should be more strict. We can be afraid that we are asking too much of our children, and then that we aren't asking enough. We may find ourselves afraid that we are too serious when we should be fun, and then too fun when we should be serious. Motherhood can be an exercise in contradictions. It can leave us feeling confused, inadequate, and frightened. The stakes are high, and mothers know it. We fear that even one shortcoming on our part will limit the potential for success a child might otherwise have. The worry that one mother-misstep can separate a child from his or her spiritual birthright can be an unbearable weight and leave us crippled with anxiety. When those moments come, remember Mary. Remember that she also was afraid.

I remember one period of my life when nearly every day was marked with anxiety and fear. I was a young mother in my late twenties with two small children and expecting a third. We were living thousands of miles away from any family in Upstate New York, where my husband was completing a surgical residency. This required him to be at the hospital, on average, eighty to a hundred hours per week. Money was stretched tighter than money can stretch, and so too was my strength. And then I was called to serve as the Young Women president in my ward. I served my husband, children, and young women as faithfully and well as I could until that third beautiful child was born, and then I found myself in a sea of anxiety. Trying to prepare lessons and minister to the girls with my little children crying at my feet made me feel like the young women got less of me than they deserved. Dragging those children, including a nursing baby, to activities and meetings when they were tired and hungry and wanted to be home with their mother made me feel like *they* were getting less of me than they deserved. My poor husband, exhausted and staggering under his own load, got virtually nothing, since there was nothing left of me to give. All of this left me feeling tremendously fearful that I could not accomplish all that God had asked me to do. I was afraid I couldn't serve in my calling in the way He needed me. I was more than afraid that I could not be the mother He would ask me to be and the wife my husband deserved. Every morning I opened my eyes and felt a flood of fear wash over me.

During that time, my mother worried about me from home. One very difficult day she called to check on me. After listening to my long list of fears yet again, she quietly reminded me of this powerful verse of scripture: "For God hath not given us the spirit of fear; but of power, and of love, and of a sound mind" (2 Timothy 1:7). I began to cling to that scripture. I knew then that God does not want us to be afraid. He certainly does not want us to be afraid of anything He has asked us to do. In particular, He does not want mothers, those who have been called to labor beside Him in His greatest work, to be fearful.

Through Gabriel's counsel to Mary, I think we can hear the Lord's gentle and reassuring voice saying to every mother, "Please don't be afraid." What I had forgotten during that time is what Mary must have held deep in her heart. She must have remembered that God was the Father of her son, and He would help her. Likewise, God is the Father of our children, and He will help each of us. He does not ask us to be perfect mothers. He only asks us to do our mortal part and then to allow Him to do the rest. In short, He asks us not to let our fear get in the way of our faith, but to go forth in *His power* and *His love* and with the wisdom of *His sound mind*.

And Mary said,
Behold the handmaid
of the Lord; be it unto
me according to thy
word. And the angel
departed from her.

—LUKE 1:38

SUBMISSION AND GLORIFYING GOD

A second characteristic we see in Mary is that she was submissive to God and sought only to glorify Him. After Gabriel finished giving her as much information about her calling as he would at that time, her submissive answer was, "Behold the handmaid of the Lord; be it unto me according to thy word" (Luke 1:38). Luke records that directly after this response, "the angel departed from her" (1:38). It was as if Mary's humble reply were all that Gabriel needed to hear. Once he knew she would submit to God's will, the rest of the details could be sorted out later. How Mary found the strength to utter such sweet words in light of what she knew she would face is astonishing. She would have known that when her pregnancy became visible, she could be stoned to death, according to Mosaic law. She must have wondered how her engagement to Joseph would be affected. Would he believe her? Would he still love her? Would her parents believe her? Or would she be left all alone? Was it even fair for this to be asked of her? Her humble response to Gabriel suggested none of these personal concerns: "Be it unto me according to thy word." Mary was concerned only about glorifying God, never about glorifying herself.

Part of our struggle as mothers sometimes may be that we forget all too easily that we are to be like Mary in this regard. Our only concern should be to glorify God, not ourselves. I learned this lesson one day as I cried to my own mother over concerns about each of my children. I was worried that they just weren't going to measure up. I worried about their performance in school and how they compared to other kids. I worried about their abilities in sports and music and whether or not any of them would excel. I worried about how their teachers and Church advisers viewed them and if they could rise as leaders. I even worried about how they fit in among their peers and whether they would be popular and well liked. And, to my shame, I worried about how their success or lack thereof reflected on me as a mother. I was convinced that somehow if I could just be an outstanding mother, they would be outstanding children.

My mother listened to me for a long time, until I had exhausted my list of concerns and I paused long enough to ask her how I could be a perfect mother so I could have perfect children. Then she lovingly began to help me see that I was putting too much importance on myself. She reminded me that my job as a mother wasn't really about me. She reminded me that these children were formed in the premortal existence with strengths and weaknesses as well as predispositions and tendencies. She also reminded me that they were created with those attributes by Father in Heaven and that He made them exactly the way He wanted them to be made for His purposes and for their missions. She reminded me that my job as a mother was not to undo all of that by resculpting them into the image that I wanted them to have. Rather, my job was to take the remarkable beings God had already created and, with His help, try to guide them into becoming the people He had designed them to be. My job was to glorify Him. When we as mothers try to glorify ourselves through the accomplishments of our children, we run the risk of creating them in our image instead of remembering they are created in God's image.

But Mary kept all these
things, and pondered
them in her heart.

—LUKE 2:19

Reverence for Revelation

A third attribute of Mary's we observe in the Nativity story is her reverence for sacred things. There are several occasions when we observe her witnessing miraculous events and quietly registering them in her heart. The first of these is her reverence toward Gabriel and his announcement. We do not have any scriptural evidence of her running off to tell all of Nazareth, Joseph, or even her parents of the great event that has taken place. This is all the more remarkable when we remember that hers was a role prophesied of by Isaiah over seven hundred years before. All Israelites would have known of the prophecy of the Messiah's birth and the virgin who would bear Him (see Isaiah 7:14). Now she knew she was *that virgin* and her child was *the Messiah*, yet we observe no declaration, no bragging. There was no vanity. In fact, the only scriptural account we have of her reaction is that after the visit with Gabriel she went "with haste" to her cousin Elisabeth, whom Gabriel had indicated was also the recipient of such a miracle, and in whom perhaps Mary felt she could confide without boasting (see Luke 1:39–40).

We witness Mary's reverence again when the baby arrived in Bethlehem and shepherds came testifying of His divinity and of their angelic visitation. These were shepherds far from Mary's home of Nazareth. She must have wondered how they knew of such events. As she marveled at the sacredness of the miracles unfolding before her, "Mary kept all these things, and pondered them in her heart" (Luke 2:19).

Similarly, some years later, when Jesus was twelve years old, His parents took Him to the temple in Jerusalem, as was the custom. On the way home, they realized He was not with them. Mary and Joseph returned to Jerusalem and found Him in the temple. Like any mother worried over a lost child, Mary asked Him why He would deal with them in that way (see Luke 2:48). When He responded that He was about His Father's business, Mary must have marveled for a moment. She must have recognized that her twelve-year-old son was not talking about the carpentry work of His earthly father, but about the work of salvation of His Heavenly Father. She must have realized in that instant that even at His tender age, He was taking on the mantle of the Messiah. Again, we do not see her making loud pronouncements or marching Him back into the temple and advertising Him and His teaching to all who would listen. Her moment of revelation is understated in the scriptures again by this familiar phrase: "His mother kept all these sayings in her heart" (Luke 2:51). And then they quietly returned to Nazareth.

As the mother of the Son of God and a uniquely special witness of Christ, Mary surely must have seen sacred things. And yet we hear nothing from her about any such moments. Whatever experiences she had between heaven and earth, she kept them quietly in her heart.

As partners with God in the rearing of children, mothers can seek and expect to receive revelation from heaven. Do we seek it? When trials come and our children struggle, and when we wonder what to do, do we fall to our knees and seek guidance from Him who loved them first? We can receive heavenly instruction and insight in all of its forms, if we will only ask. We can be blessed with vision and understanding in behalf of each child, if we will only pray. Each child is a god in embryo and, as such, deserves to be raised in reverent care by a mother who seeks tutoring from God the Father in every aspect of that child's development. He will tutor us. He will whisper sacred truths about our children that will enable us to raise them under His care. But we must keep such communication from heaven sacred. Like Mary, we must keep these things quietly in our hearts.

And the angel said
unto them, Fear not: for,
behold, I bring you good
tidings of great joy, which
shall be to all people.

—LUKE 2:10

A MOTHER'S
EXAMPLE

As we study Mary and observe her characteristics, it is not hard to imagine why Heavenly Father would have chosen her to be the mother of the Son of God. The faith, submission, and reverence we see in her are also characteristics the Savior manifests. For example, her courage to continually choose faith over fear is an attribute we see in Jesus throughout His entire life. In fact, we do not ever encounter the word *fear* or any synonym for it in any of the Savior's most difficult moments.

He felt pain, anguish, loss, and sorrow, but we do not ever read of Him exhibiting fear. Because He was mortal and experienced "pains and afflictions and temptations of *every* kind" (Alma 7:11; emphasis added), we assume He was not immune to this emotion, yet He never seemed to be found caught up in it. Perhaps that is simply because His faith was always too great. We cannot know, but what we do know is that from the time of His conception, His mother chose faith over fear. There can be no doubt that Jesus would have learned this principle at her knee.

Similarly, Mary's submission and desire to glorify God are also traits we see in the Savior's life over and over again. He submitted to the will of the Father and directed all glory to Him in every thought and deed. This was nowhere more evident than when He was suffering the unbearable pain and agony of Gethsemane. During this, the most lonely and agonizing moment of His mortal life, He cried for relief but then meekly prayed, "Not my will, but thine, be done" (Luke 22:42). In this expression of perfect submission, one can hear an echo of Mary's words thirty-three years earlier as she uttered, "Behold the handmaid of the Lord; be it unto me according to thy word" (Luke 1:38). Knowing that the Savior would live a life of submission, it is little wonder that Heavenly Father chose Mary to help teach and guide Him.

As with her faith and submission, Mary's reverence for sacred things was a very visible trait in the Savior's life. Even during His most public ministry, He made time to fast and pray and commune with His Father alone (see Luke 5:16; 6:12). Those were experiences He did not share. In fact, He admonished us to be careful that we "give not that which is holy unto the dogs, neither cast ye your pearls before swine, lest they trample them under

their feet" (Matthew 7:6). The scriptures even at-
test to numerous miracles the Savior performed
that were followed by His request that those who
witnessed these miracles were to "tell no man"
(Matthew 8:4). Even the Savior of the world, who
came to save souls in part through His miracles,
was selective about what to share and what to keep
sacred—something He surely learned, at least to
some extent, from His mother.

What I hope we, as mothers, learn from Mary
and Jesus is that we need to *be* the kind of people
God wants our children to become. It is far less im-
portant to plan the perfect family home evening or
buy all the copies of the scripture videos for your
children to watch than it is to *be* what it is you are
trying to teach them. Children learn by example.
Elder Neal A. Maxwell has said, "Your teaching
techniques will be secondary to what you are as an
individual. Your traits will be more remembered,

compositely, than a particular truth in a particular [teaching moment]. This is as it should be, for if our discipleship is serious, it will show, and it will be remembered" ("But a Few Days," address to CES Religious Educators, September 10, 1982).

I am so grateful to my own mother for knowing this truth. My father tells the story of coming home from graduate school one day to find my mother curled up in her bed reading her scriptures and marking them with a red pencil, as she has done every day of her life. Next to her, I was curled up, at three years old, with my little Book of Mormon and my red crayon, scribbling over each verse. It would be many years before I could read the scriptures, and many more beyond that before I could understand them, but I was already gaining a testimony of their worth simply because my mother loved them, and I loved her. She taught me to study and to love the scriptures without ever saying a word.

And she shall bring forth
a son, and thou shalt
call his name Jesus:
for he shall save his
people from their sins.

—MATTHEW 1:21

SUBJECT TO PAIN

Finally, one last lesson from Mary. As she and Joseph obediently took the baby Jesus, at only eight days old, to the temple in Jerusalem, she was greeted by the prophet Simeon. As the prophet foretold of Christ's glorious mission, he told Mary that "a sword shall pierce through thy own soul also" (Luke 2:35). He spoke those words to Mary, chosen above all women to bear the Son of God. Faithful, submissive, and reverent Mary would have such pain in her life? Yes, she would. I will testify that nothing causes more pain to a mother than to watch her child suffer. I would take the thorns and arrows and all the spears the world has to throw if it meant one of my children would be spared their pain. Surely no one, save God Himself, suffered as much through the Savior's life and death as did Mary. And yet she had done nothing wrong.

Sometimes, when hard things come our way, we question our worthiness and God's love for us. When the sick child you've prayed over and sought blessings for does not get well, you might think you're being punished. When the wayward child you've cried and pled and fasted for doesn't seem to be coming back, you may think you've done something wrong. When, despite the fact that you are giving everything you know how to give, you find that your children still struggle, you may think God doesn't love you. Please know nothing could be further from the truth. Sometimes it's those whom

God loves the most—Jesus and Mary and prophets and pioneers—who have been asked to endure the most. Know that when heartache comes, you are in good company—some of the best company in all of the world, in all of time.

And the child grew,

and waxed strong in spirit,

filled with wisdom:

and the grace of God

was upon him.

—LUKE 2:40